God and Love:
A Spiritual Philosophy

By Kerry B. Beach

TO ANN—
THANKS SO MUCH
FOR YOUR THOUGHTS
AND SUPPORT!

Kerry B. Beach

God and Love: A Spiritual Philosophy
Copyright 2010 Kerry B. Beach

www.KerryBeach.com

ISBN 145-3-858768

Contents

Forward:
Who I Am

The book you hold is my explanation of my own personal spiritual philosophy as it exists at the time of this writing. I have formed this set of beliefs over the course of my life, which at this point encompasses sixty-two years. It has taken most of that time for me to think through many aspects of spirituality, and to become comfortable with the beliefs I express herein.

My childhood was not at all unusual. I grew up in a middle class family in Memphis, Tennessee, with my mother and father, four siblings, older relatives, aunts, uncles and cousins, both nearby and far away. Our family was as functional or dysfunctional as any other, depending on the day and the circumstances. We all had reasonable intellect and physical capabilities, along with normal challenges and personality issues. As adults, we all have various agreements and disagreements, which is natural. While I like to think that I had my moments, in truth, my upbringing was just fairly ordinary to any outside observer.

As a child and young adult, I attended and participated in a local church. During this period, I was atypical to some extent in that I thought about the doctrines of that religion, and was struck by how many adults in my church seemed to not understand what they claimed to believe in. Many years later, I finally matured enough to understand that most humans are very conflicted about spiritual beliefs, and many simply do not think deeply about anything, especially about topics such as the nature of God, Life and the Universe. They simply look for some structure that will allow them to fit in and get along. I

1

used to find that impossible to understand or accept, which led me to quietly question just about every aspect of belief for a very long time.

I was very far along in life before I finally realized that the complaint "I don't understand!" really means "I don't accept!" Most of us have to achieve acceptance before we achieve understanding. Young idealists like me too often feel that something we perceive as wrong must be changed to right, or the universe will somehow fall apart.

After a number of years, I found that I did not really like attending church. I always felt that most people acted as if God was only present in the Church, or God expected his creations to come before him and praise him on a regular schedule. I never felt comfortable with what I perceived to be the treatment of God as a king who was modeled after typical human rulers, with emotions, whims and the corruption of power. Age and experience has helped me temper those feelings with better understanding of human behavior, and I have realized that it is natural that most humans will have a hard time thinking beyond their human framework, but of course, youth was not so tolerant.

I have felt from early in my life that God was with me, in me and around me all the time. I regularly felt God's presence in nature; I found a walk in the woods or the mountains more worshipful than many of the church services I attended. In the wide world, I had a continual sense of wonder, at least when I was not consumed with typical human problems and fears.

I have spent my life exploring, thinking, questioning, and drawing my own conclusions about spiritual issues. I have come to realize that I am somewhat naturally a philosopher, in that many of my best capabilities are based in my ability to deal with complex problems and abstract thinking.

When I was a young man, three different clergymen – two Methodist ministers and an Episcopal priest – tried to convince me to become a minister. I never felt comfortable with that idea, even though I have a natural pull to help people and to lead people. I believe that my lack of willingness for such a vocation was based in my own uncertainty in my beliefs at the time, and my perception that, too often, church leaders were expected to somehow be better than normal humans. I was not prepared to put myself in that position. Later experiences proved that I would have had a lot of trouble had I chosen to pursue a life as a minister.

During the last few years, I have begun to feel an urge to share my beliefs with others, hence the writing of this book. It is important to me that readers understand that I am not sharing these beliefs because I hope people will agree with me. I have come to understand that each person must find their own spiritual path, just as I have done. I accept and respect each person's right to their own beliefs. My hope for this book is that, by sharing my beliefs in detail, readers will be moved to think more deeply about their own beliefs, and thereby make them stronger and more comfortable in whatever spiritual philosophy they espouse.

I am not a religious scholar at any level. Neither am I expert in all the various spiritual beliefs outside of recognized religious organizations. While I have read and listened to many spiritual teachings from various authors and speakers, I have by no means covered the spectrum of such material. What I write comes from my heart, whether it corresponds to anyone's particular teachings or not.

I have always been a voracious reader, but I tend to read fast and not really remember a lot of details in what I read. I am especially bad about this with my favorite fiction. There have been times when I purchased what appeared to be a new book from an author I have previously enjoyed, only to find upon getting a chapter or two into the book that I had read the book previously. I bring this up as a manner of explanation that, in this book, I may state that someone once wrote or said a particular idea, concept or quote without being able to remember exactly who the author or speaker was. I have no intent to plagiarize or fail to credit anyone, so I apologize now should I mention something that someone else has written or spoken about without crediting that individual.

My sincere hope is that each reader find something in this book to help them examine and strengthen their spiritual beliefs. Each reader is completely free to agree or disagree with any point of my philosophy. I am still growing spiritually, and may well change my mind on one point or another as I continue to walk my path through this life experience, and beyond, although once beyond, it is unlikely I will be able to publish my new thoughts, at least not in this form.

My most humble thanks for your consideration of my book!

Chapter 1:
What is God?

I use the name "God" to refer to the Creator of the Universe, and everything in it, including the state of being we call "Life." I probably use that name because it is the name given the Creator by the Christian religious denomination I participated in as a young person.

I believe the entity or force or intellect I name God is the same such entity that most all religions and spiritual systems refer to as the creating and controlling force in the Universe. Even though others may use different names or terms, in my belief, they refer to the same entity, and that entity created them just as it created me.

It should be noted that there are still people in the world who believe in multiple gods, and even those who believe that natural forces rule their lives rather than god-like beings. I believe these people are also God's creations.

I believe God is a part of me, and of all that is – every person, animal, plant, rock, piece of dirt, grain of sand, etc. I believe God is never separate or apart from any of God's creations, and we as God's creations can never be separated from God.

Although I use the name "God" out of common practice, I remember a term used in a series of books I read many years ago that actually describes my view of God very well. The books were written by Jane Roberts, and are generally referred to as the Seth books. Roberts was an accidental medium who would go into a trance and channel a non-corporeal entity named Seth. Jane's husband, Robert Butts, transcribed the conversations with Seth, many of which occurred in front of a group of friends who met regularly with Jane and Robert. Seth always referred to the Creator as "All That Is." This phrase expresses the fact that I see God in everything and everyone.

When people ask me what the core of my belief is, I often tell them this:

"God is looking at you through my eyes, just as God is looking back at me through your eyes."

God sees what I see, hears what I hear, smells and tastes with me, feels with me, knows my thoughts and emotions, with nothing excepted or hidden. God knows the best and the worst of me automatically. God shares my highs and lows, my achievements and my failures. I have no secrets from God (and I believe that God has no secrets from me, if I ask the right question – we will discuss that in a later chapter).

I believe that God loves me without reservation, as God loves all his creations, no matter what they do or fail to do. I believe all of us are children of God, and all equally important and equally loved.

I have often observed that, as humans, we make the mistake of imagining the Creator in human terms. I realize many people reference the Bible verse in which God says he created man in his own image. I do not believe that God, who has the intellect, knowledge and power to create us as "souls" (spiritual energy beings, if you will), create physical bodies to act as vessels for us in this life experience, and create all the other myriad manifestations that provide us a stage on which to live and interact, would exist in any standard form. God can take any "form" God chooses, or be formless.

God has no boundaries or limitations, yet we commonly make the mistake of trying to model God with human limitations, such as emotions, or limited capabilities. I have always had a disagreement with the idea of a wrathful or vengeful God, a topic which will be discussed later in this book. I also have a problem with the idea that one or more of God's creations can turn against God and actually wage war on the Creator. In my mind, the entity that can create everything in the Universe can easily change, or even destroy, any of those creations at will. To have achieved the creation of us and everything we perceive, God is essentially without any limits in capability, and has nothing to fear from any of his creations.

God is all powerful, all knowing, omnipresent, and loves everything equally. We are always one with God, and can never be separated from God, because God's love is unequivocal.

God and Love: A Spiritual Philosophy

Chapter 2:
What is The Universe?

This may seem like a question with an obvious answer, such as "the physical world in which we live." While that answer is at least partially correct, I believe that God's domain is much more complex than most of us imagine.

Many of you are probably familiar with the concept of multiple universes, which theorizes that there are an infinite number of universes in existence, physically dimensioned like the universe we currently occupy, but totally separate from our universe in a physical sense. There is also the concept of parallel universes, an infinite number of physically identical universes, locked in an identical framework of a time dimension, but each one experiencing a variation in the sequence of events, so that every possible sequence of events a human could perceive and experience actually occurs in one of the parallel universes. These theories have led some to use the term "multiverse" to describe the domain containing all these different universes.

I believe both these concepts are valid and real within God's domain. I believe any universe exists simply because it is imagined by God or one of God's creations. When we imagine a different physical form or different basis for life, whether slightly or extremely different, another universe based on that imagination exists. When we imagine what might have happened if we have decided something differently in our life, a parallel universe exists. Remember, God can imagine things we have never conceived; after all, God imagined us.

God and Love: A Spiritual Philosophy

I think of the Universe as the total of God's creation throughout infinity. God exists throughout the Universe; all of God's thoughts are manifested in the Universe. The Universe as I consider it has no dimensions, or has infinite dimensions; God can create "spaces" in the Universe which are characterized by a number of perceived physical dimensions (as in three), and can also create a dimension we know as time. Other spaces within the Universe might have no dimensions or a multitude of dimensions. Any given space might or might not be constrained by a dimension of time. At our fundamental spirit level, time is not a constraint; a later chapter discusses time in great detail. Obviously, it's extremely difficult for us, living in this three-dimensional world in human bodies, to truly imagine a differently dimensioned world. God certainly has the power to imagine anything, so we need to avoid placing boundaries on God due to our own inability in our present form.

I believe we are conscious beings with an infinite existence within the universe, so God can and does give us an infinite number of frameworks within which to have a "life" experience. I will write more about that in a later chapter, so just go along with me for now. I think that it is possible, even likely, that as we develop, we are capable of creating spaces in which we and others can experience "physical" existence, adding to the richness of the Universe for the benefit of all.

Chapter 3:
What Are We?

This is perhaps one of the most important spiritual questions a human being can ponder. As each of us exists in this life experience, we "know" we are real, solid, flesh and blood. Many of us, however, sense we are more than just this magnificent machine we call our body.

There are some who believe we are just highly evolved biological specimens and our ability to reason, communicate and dream is just the result of our fantastic brains. When the body ceases to function and sustain life, our consciousness is simply snuffed out.

There are many among us who believe we have a "soul," a part of us which survives death and carries our memories and intellect on to whatever existence comes after this life. It is my observation that most people who believe they have a soul also believe we are created at the instant of conception in this life, and we live only this life, passing to the afterlife, with our fate determined by the way we lived in this life.

Some people, perhaps a large number, believe we live many lives, and that some life situations are based on our behavior in previous life situations; these beliefs involve the concepts of reincarnation and karma.

It is my belief that I am in the essence conscious energy, and that is what we refer to as the soul. I can exist in a material form in order to participate in a particular life experience, but do not depend on form for my existence. I believe my consciousness is universal and infinite (everlasting).

11

God and Love: A Spiritual Philosophy

I believe that God created my soul *in the image* of God's essence. God gave me two great gifts: existence and the ability to create. I can therefore create situations that allow me to experience all the wonders of existence, and thereby acquire knowledge so as to realize God's dream for me, to become like God. These statements lead to a lot of questions, some of which we will explore as we consider infinity and the idea of time.

So I have proposed that this universe has God and all God's creations rolling around as conscious bits of energy. Just as I believe I am always connected to, or "tuned in to" God, I believe I am also connected to, and able to communicate in some fashion with, all other conscious bits of energy that exist in the Universe, whether they be present in my current life existence or occupying themselves elsewhere at the moment. I recognize it is immensely difficult for a live human being, so focused in his or her own physical existence, to feel any sort of definite connection with all other beings, much less be aware of or understand any definite communication with all sorts of beings that cannot be physically perceived. However, I believe we are all connected, and our general inability to perceive the connections clearly is merely evidence of how much we each have to learn.

The communication with other conscious entities I just mentioned is not necessarily a targeted, conscious conversation. It is rather a sharing of emotions and thoughts. Science now believes that our thoughts, and especially our emotions, are energetic and vibrate at specific frequencies, and therefore attract similar thoughts and emotions throughout the Universe. We have much evidence that shows that particular people, such as siblings from a multiple birth, can share an almost telepathic connection even when thousands of miles apart.

Have you ever met someone for the first time and immediately felt extremely comfortable with them, as if you had just reconnected with an old, dear friend? I have had this experience many times, and I believe this is a sign that there is a connection between me and the other person that somehow transcends this life experience. I suppose this could also be extended to someone you take an instant dislike to, for no particular reason. Perhaps you have some sort of "prior" experience with that person that was unpleasant, but cannot be recalled in your current focus.

For virtually all of my life, I have had a strong focus on the physical existence, and have only rarely had what some would view as mystical, spiritual or paranormal experiences. However, I have known people who regularly have such experiences, even to the point that they have great difficulty separating their physical existence as a human from their spiritual experiences, and therefore often find it hard to integrate fully into their society.

I had a friend many years ago who had what we would refer to as interesting psychic abilities. She often told me about how she would meet others, specific people and specific spirits who were not living at the time, in her dreams. She also told me many things about me from my supposedly previous lives. At the time, I found it all very fascinating, and had no reason to disbelieve, but I could not confirm in any way anything she told me. However, when she was around us, I had definite experiences that I have never had with the same frequency and vividness. These were generally vivid dreams and out-of-body experiences, in which I was extremely aware, if not necessarily in conscious control. I realized after this period that I had actually had out-of-body experiences as a child, but of course I could not categorize the experiences as such at that age. I remembered clearly "flying" in dreams above the very tall trees bordering my yard when I was very young. Getting back to my point, my friend often found it difficult to fit in to various work and social situations, juggling the things she experienced in her mind and spirit existence with the things she experienced as a physical human.

My experience with this friend, and others I have known with similar abilities, helped convince me that we are connected with much more than just what we perceive while in this physical existence. However, being focused in our physical body does tend to make it difficult for many of us to "remember" our inherent cosmic nature, and access faculties and abilities that don't seem in line with normal human capability, in essence, psychic abilities. It is no wonder that most human beings tend to discount both the paranormal and the spiritual, and depend for their life guidance on what appears to be solid, repeatable cause and effect.

Chapter 4:
On Soul and Spirit

I have stated that I believe I am conscious energy, inhabiting my body but existing apart from it. I believe literally everything we perceive as having any amount of "life," is made from conscious energy.

Quantum physics has been exploring the nature of the physical universe at the very smallest dimensions, specifically in the sub-atomic levels. Researchers have discovered that the smallest level of existence we can comprehend appears to be an energy field, but one with "consciousness." It further appears that all matter is made from this conscious energy. It is easy for me to imagine that this conscious energy can be transformed into both animate and inanimate matter, as we perceive them, and that conscious energy can also become part of an object constructed from matter.

I believe this conscious energy that knows itself as Me is what most of us refer to as the Soul. It is the part of me that is formless and eternal, the part that existed before this life and will exist after.

Some have theorized that, when a Soul takes on a life experience, only a portion of that Soul enters into a strict focus in that life experience. Some say we each have a higher self that is the part of our Soul which remains completely in spirit form outside this framework. Some even theorize that a Soul can split it's consciousness into many different experiences simultaneously.

Note that the idea of simultaneous existence in many forms is rooted in a "time" manner of thinking; if time exists everywhere, in all aspects of creation, then the experiences of different entities in the same or different frameworks can indeed be simultaneous. On the other hand, if time only exists within frameworks of experience that utilize time as a way of ordering things, then the same entire Soul could immerse itself in many different experiences, focusing on each in sequence, and experience a specific "time" in a specific framework completely from each entity's viewpoint.

When we think of the spirit world, or we believe we are communicating with someone or something beyond this framework of existence, we could be referencing:

- Our higher self, or other facets of our own Soul;
- Other Souls who may or may not be participating in our framework or another;
- God.

Since we are all connected, and all part of the One, it does not really matter who exactly is speaking in our cosmic ear at any given time, especially since the advice is probably valuable.

As spirits, or conscious energy, you and I are always connected to every other spirit, including all those who are in this life experience with us, all those in other life experiences that we cannot perceive, and all those who are fully in spirit form and not participating in a life experience. And of course, we are always connected to God.

On Soul and Spirit

There is a quote that is attributed to Albert Einstein. It is said that he had a sign on the door to his office that included this quote:

"Called or not called, God is present."

God and Love: A Spiritual Philosophy

Chapter 5:
What Are We Here For?

With a nod to Monty Python, this is where we discuss the meaning of life (wasn't it supposedly 42?).

So far, I have told you that I believe you and I are conscious bits of energy who happen to inhabit amazing biological machines we call bodies. I have told you I believe my existence is eternal and infinite. I have told you I believe that the Creator, God, is in constant communication and sharing with me, and with you, and further that you and I are connected to each other and to every other soul in some sublime universal communion. Most likely, your obvious question is, "Why are we going through all this pain and suffering?"

It is a fundamental matter of faith I accept that God somehow has all the knowledge and capability necessary to have created all that exists, including me. Although many spiritual teachings tell us we were created perfect, with all the knowledge and capabilities we will ever need, I believe we have to learn how to tap into that perfect set of capabilities. I believe God knows we need a way to experience everything in order to learn and grow into our perfect being. In this thing we call life, God has given us a framework for experience and growth.

Consider for a moment what it means to exist as conscious energy, without a specific form. This is what I believe constitutes our eternal souls. You are aware, capable of interacting with other souls, and capable of imagining any thing or situation you wish to. That is what true creation is. I suspect God imagined us into being, and imagined all of this world we now inhabit. At one time, I theorized that, as newly created conscious beings, God recognized we needed training, and created this life framework to give us the opportunity to experience limitations, and experiment within those limitations to become educated and begin to become more like God in wisdom and love. Now I find myself wondering if perhaps God knows existence is all about interaction and becoming, and that a conscious being can never learn it all, since that being has an infinite capability to imagine. I think this debate within myself shows that none of us can ever believe we know it all, or even very much. I have strong convictions about many facets of my faith, but on the meaning of life, I am simply grateful to God that I have this framework in which to learn and grow, and I believe there is much more for me beyond this life.

There has always been much spiritual debate about the concept of free will, and it is a concept I struggled with for many years. It is a very important part of coming to terms with life. Many of my friends see free will in terms of good and bad behavior, with appropriate consequences for either. The God I know in my heart does not judge; God loves me unconditionally, and lets me judge myself, knowing that, when my focus is in spirit form, I will recognize those things I did in life that were not based in love. I believe God gave us free will precisely because, as perfect beings in his love, he understands that there is no better way for us to learn.

In our earthly endeavors, we have recognized over and over again that mankind learns much more from failure and suffering than we ever do from success and ease. God understands we can never truly destroy ourselves or one another, since we are his creations, and in our soul we are conscious energy that can never be destroyed, except perhaps by our Creator. God has given us a great gift in that he allows us to explore every possible aspect of existence while still protected by his love, for no matter how destructive we may be in this life, we can never truly destroy anything in the context of infinite and universal existence, and we can be creative in this framework in order to explore and understand our capabilities.

God also has given us a framework in which we exist and interact with others. These others also have their own free will in order to teach us that working together, and sharing love with others, is the true sublime reason for existence. It is precisely why I believe God chose to create us – so that God would have other beings to love and to interact with.

Does our growth ever end? Is there a point at which we have completely mastered our creative capacity, and essentially become the equal of God? In my view, what each of us is capable of imagining and creating is unlimited. I believe each one of us can easily spend eternity finding more to experience, and more to learn. Perhaps God knows that, by creating us, God can experience much more, and perhaps that is why God loves us so.

In summary, life is our opportunity to experience ourselves and others, to know triumphs and suffering as we choose, and to begin to realize the joy that can be ours as we come to understand God's love, in which we are all created and held.

God and Love: A Spiritual Philosophy

Chapter 6:
Life and After Life

We all know that our current life experience had a definite beginning, and will have a definite end, as viewed from this framework. We are born, we "live", and we die.

What happens after this life, and for that matter, what happened before? These are fundamental questions that all versions of faith seek to answer, since there is no scientific way we can answer these questions, at least not with any certainty, while we are alive.

Some believe we become conscious at the instant of conception, while some believe it happens somewhere between conception and birth. Some, like me, believe we are already conscious spirits who choose a body to be born into, and by so doing choose the circumstances of their life.

A common belief in faith is that we suffer during life to prove ourselves worthy of an eternal reward after life, commonly referred to as Heaven. This belief usually goes hand-in-hand with a concept of God as wrathful and judgmental, one to be feared, and praised whenever possible in order to obtain a positive judgment. An obvious question then becomes, what is the consequence of a negative judgment? From that, we develop our various concepts of Hell.

Those who believe that we have no history before conception and birth may or may not believe in an afterlife. If one does not believe in an underlying creative intelligence such as God, then one will generally decide that death is the extinction of one's consciousness. To me, it is illogical to believe in an afterlife but not believe in some sort of God concept.

You may find it interesting that I use logic in this context. Just as an aside, I believe that logic is always operative. However, in any given situation, logic can only be determined within the scope of our knowledge. This is precisely why someone who focuses on a rigid scientific explanation for life as the result of an amazing coincidence of various chemical reactions must conclude that death, the destruction of the body, also destroys consciousness. To believe in an afterlife, one must conclude that there is some mechanism, force or intellect that makes the afterlife possible, since we obviously don't have the capability as living humans to do that.

It is my sense of logic that has led me to question common beliefs all my life, but in my logical view, there are many things in existence that are not measureable or perhaps even apparent to us while we exist in this life. My sense of logic tells me that just what we know of our selves and our universe is far beyond random chance. If God can imagine all of this, then there is no limit to God's creative capability, or ours.

Getting back on track, the beliefs I have spoken of concerning an afterlife are often accompanied by a belief in a single life experience only. There is a body of thought in faith that maintains the possibility, or even certainty, of multiple lives. I am referring to ideas of reincarnation. Many believe that we each have lived before, and will live again. Many of these also believe that our experience in this life is determined by how we lived (thoughts, words and actions) a past life, and how we live now will affect what sort of life we will have next (the concept of karma).

Life and After Life

Many also believe that each of us has a specific plan or program concerning what it is we are here to accomplish. This is often referred to as dharma, although dharma most accurately appears to mean living according to one's righteous purpose, or according to the spiritual laws.

Many reincarnation beliefs also include the spirit experiencing life as something other than a human being, generally as an animal of some sort, which can even be viewed as a reward or punishment, depending on what sort of esteem the believer holds for the particular animal.

Having listed beliefs that are common in our world and its history, now let me tell you my beliefs about these subjects.

I believe that we are spirit beings having a life experience while we are occupying these bodies.

I believe that we are eternal beings, existing for an infinite span. I believe that time as we perceive it is really an attribute of this life framework that we are all participating in.

In an earlier chapter, I spoke of multiple universes and parallel universes. This particular life framework is one that we have all agreed to collectively inhabit in order to cooperate in our learning experiences. I believe that we all actually imagined this framework, perhaps with God's active participation, and that we continue to imagine it as we live in it. I further believe that we can easily imagine the same framework with each decision point spinning off a copy with a different sequence of events – parallel universes.

God and Love: A Spiritual Philosophy

I believe that we, again perhaps with God's help and participation, are capable of imagining a multitude of entirely different life frameworks, with vastly different physical rules. An infinite number of universes, and therefore an infinite number of potential life experiences, are well within the capability of God and his creations. What else would we do with an infinite existence?

I also believe that we consciously choose what experiences, or at least what circumstances, we want from each life. These choices are made by us in our spirit guise, the level of our soul, before we enter a particular life experience. I also believe that free will gives us the ability to change those intentions at any point in our life experience. I believe that, while our own consciousness may make us susceptible to the concepts of karma and dharma, we are not slaves to these ideas, except perhaps if we strongly believe in them.

While we may well generate a sequence of events on a spiritual level, time as we perceive it now is merely an attribute of this life. Outside of a life experience, at least this one, we do not mark time as a linear dimension. We do not grow or age, we simply are, with all our capabilities. If that is true, why do we have life experiences, with all the attendant problems?

For a moment, consider yourself as an all-knowing being, an all-powerful being who is capable of imagining any circumstance into personal reality. You can think up anything, but you have to do all the thinking. You have to construct the entire situation, and script every action and event. You find yourself craving surprise and uncertainty, and especially, another intellect to interact with. It's terribly boring to just hang around in the void, even if you have other spirit friends to hang with, so you and your spirit friends begin making plays, vastly creative affairs which engage your creative capabilities and present you with situations you haven't thought of. It's delicious, and much better than hanging around just being you.

I believe what we are doing now is what we will do for the rest of eternity. We will indulge in all sorts of experiences, in order to learn how to interact with other beings who are truly equal to us – in order to become more like God, and fulfill the promise of his creation. I believe every one of us has the ability to choose our path throughout eternity, and can choose to hang for a while in spirit, or dive right back in to another life experience.

So what of Heaven and Hell? I believe we make our own Heaven or Hell, based on our beliefs, and we can do so in whatever experience we happen to be having, such as right here.

So what happens when we die? We have all read or heard about near-death experiences, what people experience when they are dying or are clinically dead, but who are brought back by heroic medical action or miraculous events. Most of these descriptions speak of a white light and an unbelievable feeling of love, although I am aware of at least one person who saw and felt flames, the common concept of Hell.

I believe we each will experience the moment of death and immediate moments after according to our specific beliefs. I definitely believe that, if one is fearful of going to Hell, one may actually create a hellish experience at first in order to satisfy that strong, fearful belief. However, I do not believe God will allow someone to continue to suffer as a spirit just to satisfy an erroneous belief. Because you have free will, God will allow you to create, for an instant, the experience you are expecting. Then God will whisk you back into his love and help you to understand why you were afraid and feeling unworthy.

It occurs to me many people will argue with this view, on the basis that they or others have experienced dark or evil spirits in this life. If you believe in such entities, even just a bit, and especially if you have a fear of such happenings, you have the power to create them in your reality, and when that happens, they will be very real to you. Even if you cannot banish these fears and beliefs yourself, God can, whether here in this life because you ask him to, or outside of this life, when all he has to do is explain to you how those terrible experiences were manifested according to your beliefs.

So we are born, we live, we die, we feel the welcoming, enveloping love of God, we see our other kindred spirits again for a while, and then we decide what to do with ourselves next, on and on for infinity – endless adventure!

Chapter 7:
On Time and Eternity

What is time, really? Fundamentally, time is an exquisite way of creating a sequence for all events that occur. If we had no clocks, then we would simply recognize a sequence of occurrences. We would identify a particular event as having happened before another, but after a third event. We would be able to describe the sequence of events, but not precisely, and we would not be able to place the desired event properly in the sequence of all events that have ever occurred, should we care to do so.

Would you or me or someone else really care about the relationship of occurrence of our interesting events and everybody else's interesting events? We probably would not care about all events, but we might care enough about some subset of events that involve others. For instance, again with no clock, we might set out to do four things, and decide that a sequence of A, B, C and then D would serve our purpose. However, if C was the event "Meet Larry for lunch at the diner," we might then decide to do the sequence A, B, D and then C, and we would also now become concerned about being able to complete A, B and C so that we can meet Larry for lunch. Oh, now we have another problem – how do we know that we will arrive for the lunch precisely when Larry arrives, rather than long before or long after.

Here in this earthly physical existence, we operate in a constrained manner, forced by our very physicality to perform most tasks sequentially. In order to efficiently interact with other spirits who are also living physically, we need some mechanism to allow us to plan and synchronize our tasks, events and interactions, so God (and we) invented the concept of time. Having been invented, time took on the aspects of a dimension – *when* became just as significant as *where* in our experience.

Most people treat time as a universal constant, and it is very easy for us to synchronize our thinking, and therefore our recognition of time, in a manner that makes time appear to be not only constant but immutable. However, I have experienced many moments when time personally slowed down in my perception, and enabled me to do things that I never thought I could do. Let me share some examples.

Through my life, I have been what many people have termed a "natural" athlete, meaning that I have very good coordination, fine motor skills, and fast reflexes. I realized early on that, at times when I needed to respond extremely quickly, my perception of events became so acute that I actually perceived things moving slower than normal, and was able to move my body quickly enough to make the play, avoid the blow, or successfully manage whatever situation I was reacting to. This has happened frequently in sports, in driving, and just in everyday activities. Even now in my sixties, when I am no longer as athletically capable as I was, I still experience this effect of slowing time when needed. I believe that many others experience it to, but just don't think about it as much as I have.

That's not the only way that I have experienced time becoming malleable. When I was attending college, I worked in television production and on-air operations as a broadcast engineer. Because every event was scheduled to the second, it was vital that everything we did started and ended exactly on the prescribed times, or at least as close as we could make it. I quickly learned that one second could often seem to me as if it were several seconds, especially if we had come out of something early and were left with "dead air" – no sound and blank or static video. We had large analog clocks with sweep second hands everywhere, all synchronized, to help us coordinate all the bits and pieces, so we would often glance at the nearest clock and sync in before we pushed whatever button was called for next, to be sure it was pushed at exactly the right time. I found repeatedly that, when I looked at the clock, it would seem to stop moving for at least a second, and then suddenly start moving again at its normal speed, even though the mechanism would never work that way. I still have that experience often when I look at a clock that displays seconds.

So why does this happen, when we know that our various timekeeping machines operate at a constant speed by design? Does my brain suddenly change the manner in which it processes the information, so that I experience an illusion that time has slowed down, or is the truth that time is the illusion, and we make time seem constant by the way we perceive it. I vote for the latter interpretation.

Now consider that you are fully back into your spirit self, existing outside of any specific life framework. You are constantly hooked into the spiritual communications network, so that you can synchronize at will with any other spirit that you wish to. Further, consider that you are truly unlimited in your ability to imagine any situation or circumstances you wish to immerse yourself in, sort of like being able to have amazingly vivid dreams at will. If you want to communicate with other spirits who are having life experiences, you can simply "dial in" to that spirit at a specific point in that spirit's experience, whenever you want to. You might communicate with that spirit who is in physical form three times, each time in a different life experience for that spirit. Or three times in the same life experience, but at times that are widely separated for the spirit who is bound by time. However, for you, these three communications events happen right after each other, in sequence.

In truth, these ideas of being outside of the dimension of time are just as hard for me to imagine and describe as they are for you to read and imagine. I am certain that real spiritual reality, outside of a physical life experience, is much stranger, and much richer, than any one of us can imagine while we are here in our bodies. It's one of those things for which you just have to be there to understand.

The point I am trying to make is that, in my belief, there is no limit to our true spiritual nature, our God-like form. We may adapt a sequential mode of operation as a convenience, so that we can order ourselves and our activities, but even then, we are not bound to a specific rate of ordering. While in spirit form, any and all of an infinite number of life frameworks and life experiences are available to us. We can check in, be a spectator, give guidance, or even decide to participate, perhaps picking up again at some decision point in one of our "past" lives to see how it plays out when we decide differently.

Yes, I think we can choose to re-enter a life at a point after birth. Of course, if we do that, we have to re-enter it with the state of mind that we had at that point. We can't go back and consciously "know what we know now." I am getting a bit off track for the topic of this chapter, so I apologize.

On Time and Eternity

It may be that many spirits choose to follow a semi-time discipline in their spirit form for convenience sake, but if they do, that semi-time is, in my belief, highly malleable.

To summarize, I believe that time is an aspect of this life experience, and probably many others, but not an aspect of existence in the entirely spiritual realm. I also believe that spirits are everlasting, and able to touch all "times." While a spirit may gather more knowledge and therefore grow by experiencing events sequentially, a spirit never ages as a physical body does, since a spirit has no form, and can imagine any form it wishes at any moment.

The concept of infinity as applied to time simply means "never-ending." Infinity is not as overwhelming if you do not have to mark time. A belief that we are ever-lasting, never-ending and infinite must also imply that we never get tired or bored, that there are an infinite number of things to experience and learn. I believe that is so. With that belief, I can truly predict that I have met or will meet every one of you somewhere along the way. Watch for it!

God and Love: A Spiritual Philosophy

Chapter 8:
All You Need Is Love

I believe there is only one rule in God's universe – all you need is love (thanks, John Lennon).

As humans, we have spent way too much time and energy making up all sorts of rules, and caused too much pain and suffering to ourselves and others in the process. I believe that, if every being practiced love for every other being, our need for all those other rules would melt away.

I am not such an idealist to expect to see everybody loving everybody tomorrow, or anytime soon. However, I do my best each day to treat everyone with love, in all situations. I don't always succeed, but I try.

To me, the easiest way to automatically think love for another person is to recognize that the other person shares the same relationship with God you and I do. Everyone is our brother or sister in Creation. If we are to live as love and in love, we then automatically live The Golden Rule.

How can we show love in every situation? Those of us who have gathered any small amount of wisdom know too well that there are always situations we can't cure, change, or cause to become positive. The human experience seems to always involve very negative, tragic, and even evil occurrences and circumstances, and none of us are immune to such experiences. What we must strive to do is to avoid judgment of the people involved, recognizing that they are acting according to their beliefs, no matter how misguided those beliefs may be. Seek to have compassion and forgiveness for all who have strayed from, or not yet found, their way to universal love.

I know many of you are now thinking there are some behaviors and events that cannot possibly be forgiven. You may also complain that there are times when each of us must make a hard choice, to either do something horrible to someone else or experience a horrible thing done to ourselves or someone we care for. I have never been involved in combat, but I can imagine how difficult it must be for one person to purposely kill another. It is also obvious to me that any given human is quite capable of killing another, or worse, given certain circumstance and beliefs.

As painful as large-scale bad events seem, they serve a purpose for both individuals and for societies. Just as each individual learns valuable lessons from bad experiences, so too do large groups of people. We certainly do not, as individuals, organizations, or societies, wish tragic experiences on others. If we are the best we can be, we respond to these events with love and compassion. However, we also must accept that good comes from every occurrence, no matter how terrible it seems, and we must look for the good.

When I think about unhappy events and unhappy circumstances, I strive to remember two truths. The first of these is, I learn the most valuable lessons by experiencing adversity, as do we all. I cannot expect to be able to go through a life experience without making mistakes and being challenged. If my mistakes are few and not particularly harmful, then I am very fortunate indeed, but I may also have learned very little.

All You Need Is Love

The second truth I remember is that each spirit participating in life has their own plan, and free will to exercise or change that plan. I may have to be part of several other's plans that may be painful to me. I believe that, on a spiritual level, I have my own free will to decide whether to participate in other's experiences, but in my human form, I am not always capable of conscious knowing regarding those choices. I remind myself that I cannot really harm that spirit, no matter what damage I may do to their earthly personification. This is not an excuse for bad behavior, but rather an acceptance of the fact that I may be called on to play a difficult role, and have seemingly no way to avoid that role.

It can be said that there is generally an ultimate way to avoid a distasteful role, that being to remove oneself from this thread of life. I have a very hard time imagining what would cause me to do that.

I choose to go forward in life with love in my heart for each and every being, for all of God's creation, forgiveness for any hurt caused to me, and the promise only to make the best choice I can at each step along the way.

God and Love: A Spiritual Philosophy

Chapter 9:
On Religion and Churches

I attended the United Methodist Church when I was young, up through my teenage years. Even though my maternal grandfather was a life-long Methodist preacher, my family was not particularly religious. My mother was more concerned about church attendance than my father, although she did not attend all Sundays. My mother did try to interest us in going, especially when we were very young, so I did go through the Sunday school classes over many years, eventually joining the church as a teenager and becoming the youth leader for a while.

I should note that I was fortunate to have a mother who exposed me to religion but left me free to make my own choices regarding it. Many of my friends became members of their parent's churches or religions because it was expected, and encountered problems later as adults when they wanted something different.

Two very interesting things happened to me during that time as a Methodist youth leader. Because of my position, I was a member of the church board and attended board meetings. This was during the 1960's in Memphis, Tennessee, a time of great racial tension and civil rights struggles. Typical of the South in that time, there were no black people in membership or in attendance at my church. Our pastor asked the board what he should do if black people tried to attend any of our services. To my absolute amazement, one of the kindest elderly ladies in our community declared strongly that she would not allow those people in "her" church. She used a term which I will not repeat here. I was the only member of the board to point out that they were people just like us. I was only sixteen or so at the time, and was kindly dismissed and ignored as being too young to understand.

Yes, I was a young idealist, and I had many experiences during my youth and young adulthood in which I found it difficult to reconcile the ideas of equality for all, as did most of our population. However, that one episode was, I think, the beginning of my exploration of my inner self as I related to religion and belief. That was the seed that led me to seek God in my own heart and in the world at large, rather than in some building on Sunday morning. Over the years that followed, I often took note of the seeming hypocrisy of the various people I met in the several churches I attended.

I met my bride-to-be just before going off to my first year of college. When we married a bit over two years later, she had joined the Episcopal Church, and wanted to be married by her priest. I therefore became confirmed as an Episcopalian. We moved very soon to another town, and attended an Episcopal church there, but found ourselves very disappointed with the priest and the membership there. We stopped attending church for several years, then eventually joined a Methodist church in Garland, Texas, where a friend of ours was the pastor. When my career put us on the move again, we ceased having a membership in any church. During this time, my idealism continued to be at the forefront of my thinking, and of course I found more to be unhappy about, as I continued to see that the average person rarely thought about what they claimed to believe.

During these years, there were three times in my life when ministers attempted to convince me that I should join the clergy. The first was my Methodist minister at the church I attended as a teenager. He was a nice man, but I remember his daughters more than I remember him; that's probably a reflection of where my mind was at that time.

The second invitation came from the Episcopal priest who married us. He was a very charismatic man, and I could easily see why my wife was attracted to his church. I was quite surprised when he tried to convince me to consider the priesthood.

The third was the pastor of the Methodist church in Garland. His wife was a flutist, as is my wife, and they played and taught together. We all became good friends, which is why we attended that church. When he spoke to me about becoming a minister, I told him I had already had two other invitations, and I felt such a position was not where my path lay.

In all three of these invitations, I obviously recognized I had serious misgivings about religion in general, at least given what I had experienced, which was protestant Christianity. Over the following years, I would gain some understanding of non-Christian religions from my military service and just making a wider range of acquaintances. I spent a year on remote assignment in Alaska, and some of my best friends there were a Hawaiian family who followed the Baha'i faith. That was a very interesting experience, and like so many when encountering something exotic, I thought about joining. In the end, though, I continued to feel that my path lay elsewhere.

Years later, we tended to spend our Sundays hiking in the Shenandoah Mountains, and simply left behind the idea of church membership or attendance. My wife, being a free-lance

41

musician, played at many churches whenever she could get a paying gig, and got to enjoy the ritual and formality in that way, which I believe was what drew her to Episcopalians in the beginning.

I am in no way implying that my wife's view of religion and churches is the same as my own. This book is about my views, and while she has lovingly accommodated my views, she may have different ideas.

Having given you all this background, it's about time I finally detailed my views on this subject!

Throughout my years, I have looked for God in nature, in people, and in my own heart, and I have found God in all those places. I learned long ago to listen to my thoughts to uncover my beliefs about spirituality, and I believe that I have received guidance from God at times during that internal debate. I have recently recognized that, while I was listening carefully to my self talk about spirituality, I should have also been listening to my self talk about everything else. Had I done so, I might have saved myself and my family some of the financial problems we have experienced. On the other hand, those experiences have been learning experiences, and were probably necessary on some level.

Getting back to churches and religions, my idealism has mellowed tremendously over the years. I now understand that most people are drawn to religious participation for all sorts of social reasons, from a heavy family and peer expectation to a desire to be part of a community. It is interesting that I felt repelled by the doctrine, even though I have always loved being with people, even becoming a leader in various community and professional organizations throughout the years when we had children at home.

I now understand that my problem is primarily with religions, or religious institutions. I have found that many churches are very beneficial social organizations, give much meaning to their members, and in some cases do great good in their communities. Many churches bring communities and people together.

Sadly, the history of most of the world's great religions contains terrible acts against people, and even today, religion tends to be the major reason for tension and combat amongst many in this world. I believe this is the fundamental reason that religions are finding their memberships waning, and many large churches have become essentially independent. I do see the world population as a whole becoming more awake to spirituality, with more and more people searching for their own spiritual path. That is, in fact, the primary reason I decided to finally say yes to that small voice telling me to write my book.

My guiding principle is that every human being must find his or her own spiritual path, and each path is likely very unique to each person. If you find your path in an established church or religion, or as I have in my own study and reflection, then practice your beliefs to the best of your ability but never stop thinking about them and questioning them. That process will only make you stronger and wiser, and a better member of both the spiritual and physical worlds.

God and Love: A Spiritual Philosophy

Chapter 10:
On Human Relationships

Unless you are a successful hermit, life involves numerous relationships with other human beings. Most people find relationships frequently challenging.

Relationships have always been important to me, and have often been challenging for me. I like being with people, especially friends with whom I share some sort of common interest. I like meeting new people, which is what drew me to work like real estate, and is now drawing me to teaching and coaching. I also have a tendency to want to lead when I am in groups, and I have seen the relationship change when my friends became my employees and team members.

I have been blessed to have a relationship with my spouse that has lasted over forty years, but we have had to work at it many times, which is normal for most marriages, and for most any kind of relationship beyond a casual acquaintance.

Given my belief that we are all one in and with God, I see every other human being as truly my brother or sister, my fellow "child of the universe," if you will. That does not mean that I find it easy to interact with every person I meet. Each person is their own being at some point in their path, and their "vibration" at that point may not be compatible with mine. As I have grown, both spiritually and physically, I have become more likely to feel love and compassion for someone even as I understand that a close relationship is unlikely. I do always try my best to be considerate of each person I interact with.

God and Love: A Spiritual Philosophy

With my friends, I have always been very open about my feelings, and this has sometimes caused misunderstandings. I have learned to be more conscious of how my "expression," meaning not just my words but also my actions, may be interpreted by others, depending on the context of the moment. I have learned to be careful about subjects such as religion and politics!

These last few paragraphs are included just to show that my experience with relationships has been fairly normal. Now let me address relationships further according to my spiritual beliefs.

I have already pointed out that I see every other human being as part of me and part of God. In that context, each one is precious to me. However, each one is living a life experience for their own reasons, just as I am, and each is entitled to follow their own path through that experience. This last point, by the way, includes my children. I might want to be everybody's friend, but that is highly unlikely. What I try to do is give every one I interact with whatever they need from me, with love and respect.

I have often been intrigued by the possibility that I have special connections to certain other people. I am sure that most of you have had the experience of meeting a stranger and feeling like you knew that person very well already, that you were somehow drawn together by some shared "thing" on a very deep level. I have had this experience many times.

Some theorize that such a connection is an indication of a past life relationship, and I have in fact had friends in the past who believed exactly that. Another theory could be that the people who feel that connection are actually "facets" of the same spiritual being. Remember that, in earlier chapters, I talked about parallel universes and multiple life experiences. While the idea of one spirit occupying two or more life experiences in the same life framework at the same time is somewhat more difficult to consider, in truth, there is no reason why this could not be. This idea also supports the idea of a spirit keeping part of his or her consciousness purely in spirit form (the "higher" self), while the rest of the consciousness participates in life experiences.

If we are all connected spiritually, there could be many reasons that we feel a connection in life. As I have already shared, I do believe that we each live many life experiences, perhaps an infinite number. I am certain that my spirit has not always been a white male in every human experience, and I also suspect that there are many other life frameworks besides bipedal humans of two sexes. I do believe that, as spirits in cooperation with God, we are unlimited in our imagination and creativity, so we can construct an infinite number of life frameworks with which to experiment.

We already know that our current world contains a rich diversity of what it means to be human. While we tend to think of certain expressions of life as "normal," in reality it's the people who live outside of those approved expressions that lend a spice to the world. Our life experience would be dull indeed if we were all the same, both physically and philosophically. Never be sorry to encounter someone who is atypical, for they can be a wonderful learning experience, and they are also a member of your spiritual family, perhaps even another expression of you.

God and Love: A Spiritual Philosophy

.

Chapter 11:
On Abundance

As I write this, I am embarked on my own quest to manifest abundance. We have all been conditioned to measure abundance in financial terms, since in our society, money is the tool by which we have freedom to pursue just about whatever we desire. For me, money is key because I am in deep debt at this time, the result of never really understanding my "programming," the beliefs I have held for so long at a non-conscious level. I won't go into my own manifestation quest here; that is probably a subject for another book.

Instead, I want to focus on what abundance really means. I have come to believe that true abundance means giving whatever your gift is to the world. We each have one or more gifts that make us unique among individuals. Some maintain that we come into each life with a specific purpose, but many of us forget that purpose because we fall prey to the negativity of our world. A purpose could be the giving of a special gift, as in doing something that somehow benefits others, or it could be simply having a specific experience in order to learn and grow. Having an experience may still be a gift to others, for creating an experience often requires the cooperation of many people. Either way, I do believe that each of us has some role to play in this life.

Some teachers believe that, because of free will, we can and do fail to fulfill our role in a given life experience, and have to try again if that role has particular meaning to us as spirits. This may well be true. However, I believe that many people give their gift in small ways, while others give theirs in a big way. It may be that we have to start small and work up to being big.

God and Love: A Spiritual Philosophy

In any event, whatever our gift is, whatever our purpose is for being here, giving that gift is what empowers us and creates our individual abundance.

Many of you are probably wondering what any of this has to do with having it all? Nothing, and everything.

Particularly in the western world, we are conditioned to equate the term abundance with lots of money and material possessions, and the ability to do whatever we wish to do with our time and energy. This can certainly be part of a specific individual's abundance, but as we all know, having great financial wealth does not guarantee fulfillment of one's dreams, or any sense of peace and contentment. Sadly though, too many people believe that peace and joy are in opposition to wealth, which is definitely not true.

Each of us has a situation which, when fully engaged, will bring us to a state of full realization of our true selves, a state of peace, joy, even bliss. For each of us, that state is unique, and is related to whatever our gift or purpose is. We may achieve it in life, or we may not, but we have the power to achieve it, no matter what our seeming circumstances, if we only can understand it and believe in it. God wants nothing more for us than to blossom into who we really are. We can have whatever material things we want in life, but all of that stays here. When we are in spirit, all we have is our experiences and our relationships with the other spirits we have interacted with.

So what good comes from material wealth? If you use your material wealth to further your gift or purpose, it becomes a tool for great good. If your focus is simply acquisition instead of enabling, then material wealth serves little purpose, in my opinion.

Let's move beyond material abundance, and recognize that an abundance of time, health, love, joy, etc. is just as important, or perhaps even more so, than financial or material abundance. Let me be clear: do not fear material wealth, do not be afraid to envision it for yourself, but do not let yourself focus only on the material.

I believe that the most important part of making a heaven on earth is the relationships that one has with others. We all probably have known someone who needed very little of material wealth because he was very wealthy in love and friendship. As has been said many times by many others, we come into this world with nothing, and we leave it the same. My modification of that saying is that we come into this world with only a reason, and we leave it enriched by the other lives we touched, or with regrets for having missed the opportunities.

The truth of the Law of Attraction is that we can be whatever we believe ourselves to be. We can have an abundance of whatever we want, for whatever reason; we have the ability to create that for ourselves. We will find our highest joy when we find our true selves and show ourselves, unique and shining, to the world.

God and Love: A Spiritual Philosophy

Chapter 12:
On Finding Your Own Way

As a young person, I was exposed to religion, but not pushed hard into it, which was probably a good thing, given the questions that I came up with regarding religion and God. Over the many years of my life, I have focused on finding my own way to my spiritual philosophy. I have met many others who have also, to a greater or lesser extent, questioned what society offered them and found their own spiritual path, even while they participate in an established religion. If you are wondering how to find your path, I will offer a description of how I have come this far, and perhaps a suggestion or two to help you along your way.

I am by nature an analytical person. I think about things, often very deeply, when those things are important to me. It is instructive to note that, if something is not particularly important to me at the moment, I may not give it any significant amount of thought, which is why I have negative and limiting beliefs just like everybody else, and why I can easily make a mistake, just like everybody else. I am really no different than you, and if you are willing to question each and every thing that pertains to whatever subject you want to get clear on, you can find your way in any matter.

In my youth, religion troubled me. I readily saw a lot of hypocrisy in the religious practice of the people around me, and that really bothered me. As I thought further, I begin to see aspects of religious teaching and church doctrine that did not ring true to me. Many of my questions were based on feelings I had when something just did not seem to ring true. I have attempted to explain many of those conflicts and my conclusions in the previous chapters, and I hope I have been clear on specific points.

As I went deeper, I had to consider carefully everything I read, saw and heard, and even every thought I had, and really ask myself if whatever I expressed in my mind really matched with my view of God, the universe and life. If I found something lacking, I had to ponder why, and try to construct a scenario that made sense of all my feelings. I could never accept that the God who created all of us and all that we can perceive could be anything but a being of love. I could also never accept that, having created such wonder, that this all-knowing and all-powerful being would destroy even a small part of it.

My arguments were actually quite logical, at least to me, and they still are. What I have found most interesting in my older age is that, even while I was purposely examining everything in one certain category with a microscopic attention to detail, I was simply absorbing all sorts of subconscious programming in other areas. In the last several years, as I have confronted mediocrity and lack of success in my working life, I have had to turn the harsh spotlight on all those other beliefs and feelings stored inside my mind, and try to make sense of them.

Now, I am becoming more conscious and aware about all aspects of my life. I am examining each and every thought, and asking myself whether that thought provides love and support to myself and others, or if that thought limits me and withholds love.

I am striving to become truly aware of not only all my thoughts and actions, but also each and every bit of God's universe that I interact with, especially the people and spirits I come in contact with. I am working to make a habit of giving love, understanding and compassion to all, helping in whatever way I can, and blessing those whom I cannot reach at this time.

I am also remembering to have love and compassion for myself, accepting my self in all aspects. This is, for many people, the hardest thing to do, but it is the most essential. You cannot give to another what you cannot give to yourself.

I have become better at hearing those thoughts and happenings that are communications from God and spirit to help guide me. By being more aware and open, and not dismissing anything that I perceive, I now hear and see much more than I used to.

See how easy it is? You just have to be willing to let go of most everything you have learned, especially all your non-conscious programming. You have to be willing to figure out what your purpose or gift is, and be willing to give that gift at every opportunity. You must also be able to allow others to be themselves, no matter what their state of knowing is, and bless them with love and understanding, because they are all your family. It is not easy, but it is who you truly are.

It is not easy, but you don't have to do it all at once, or even in a hurry. Start as I did, focusing on one aspect, your spiritual path, because that is the core that will enable all other aspects of your being. I am confident that, as I give my gift by writing this book and helping others, the other aspects of my self and my life will become what I would like them to be, as long as I am willing to be present, with intent, to all that I am at all times.

God and Love: A Spiritual Philosophy

Chapter 13:
On (Inner) Peace

I have spoken to you about recognizing God in yourself and in all others. I have told you that I believe we are all perfect but just inexperienced, and subject to lots of pressures that are part of our life experiences. I have told you I believe we all must have both good and bad experiences in order to learn and grow. If there is one thing we all should strive for, that thing is peace, in our selves and amongst our selves. I believe peace must begin in each of us.

A very wise man recently said that true inner peace is characterized by a complete lack of judgment. I think this may well be the most difficult state for a human being to achieve. All our lives, we are confronted with judgment. Our very idea of justice is based on judging the actions of others. If we are to truly live without judgment, then we must accept every action, no matter how vile, forgive the source of that action, and look for the good.

We must also forgive ourselves for everything we have done that we are ashamed of. We must forgive our family and friends for every time they slighted us, or made us feel unloved and unwanted. We must trust that even the worst criminal holds within a bright and shining soul that comes from God.

It is a hard thing to do for anyone, but only when we can all find true inner peace will the world know true peace.

Start with yourself. Forgive yourself for all those attitudes, habits, past actions, thoughts, etc. that are less than you want to be. Release all judgments you have of yourself. Accept yourself as you are, and remember God created you in perfection, and loves you unconditionally. Love yourself as God loves you.

Now, extend your love to your family. Forgive them for all the things that made you sad, resentful and hurt. Forgive them for whatever it is or was that has brought pain and distance to your relationships. Accept them as your family, both in life and in creation, spirits who are truly one with you and with God. Release all judgments you have of each of them, and love them as God loves them and you.

Do the same for all your friends and coworkers, in every aspect of your life. Recognize their spirits as a part of you in God. Think further, to all beings and all things in this Universe, and recognize that they too are part of your family. All people are your brothers and sisters. All of God's creation is a part of your consciousness, linked to you for all eternity through God.

Strive always to give up judgment, give love, and practice the Golden Rule, my brothers and sisters, and we will all have Peace.

A Final Word

I am under no illusion or conceit that I have all the answers. In fact, I do not think anyone residing in human form has all the answers, even the "old souls" present among us. It truly seems there is a veil that is drawn for most of us when we are born that separates us from the knowledge of our spirit form, so that we can fully experience this life. So question and learn, be secure in the knowledge that you are doing your best, and always be open to new information or feeling, while maintaining a healthy skepticism. I believe if you do that, your guidance will also be delivered.

As I have written this book, in summer of 2010, there is an awakening taking place throughout the world. More and more people are questioning their way of life, becoming more conscious of how they interact with the world around them, and hopefully becoming more aware of how they relate to spirit. Many believe that we are about to enter what may be a golden age for humanity on Earth. I believe that this opportunity is real, and have committed myself to play whatever part is mine to play in this movement. This book is the first contribution; I sincerely hope that there will be many other contributions to come.

My mission, at least for the short term, is to directly touch and positively affect the lives of at least one million people by the end of 2012, and to be a voice to the world for living in spirit, consciousness and abundance. In the longer term, I want to be part of helping the world become a much better place for everyone – more peaceful, more loving, more supportive. I want us to become much better stewards of this planet that provides us such a miraculous place to experience and grow. I want to see a world where everyone can understand their unique value, and can give their gift to everyone they touch. Many may see that dream as impossible, but I know in my heart that it can come true.

I sincerely hope that each of you has found value in something I have written here. If so, please let me know, for I will be truly honored. Know that each of you are loved, by God, and by me. Thank you!

Made in the USA
Charleston, SC
05 November 2010